What a Machine!

Lalie Harcourt & Ricki Wortzman

Illustrated by John Weissmann

Dominie Press, Inc.

Chapter 1: Harry Plans!

Everyone in town knew that Harry loved to make things. So no one at the town meeting was surprised when Harry offered to make breakfast for the Fun Fair. But they **were** surprised when he said that he didn't need any help. Making breakfast for hundreds of people is a big job.

"No problem," said Harry. "I have an idea."

Harry loved to solve problems — the bigger the problem, the better. Harry left the meeting as soon as he could. He was very excited about the idea that he had started to think about.

When Harry got home, he started to make plans. The Fun Fair was in one week. One week was not a lot of time! Harry wasn't worried about being ready in time, but he didn't want to have to rush. Harry hated to rush. He liked to take his time and do things right.

Harry drew his plan. He made a list of things he needed. He made a schedule of what he would do each day. Harry was ready to put his plan into action. He started by going to bed on time.

Chapter 2: Harry Gets Busy

On Saturday morning, Harry left the house after eating a good breakfast. He needed cans and bottles for his plan. Harry knew just where to go. He just hoped that he wasn't too late.

Harry was happy to find what he needed so quickly. He went home to clean the cans and bottles. He cleaned and cleaned until the cans and bottles looked like new. He liked to make old things look new again. Harry was pleased that his plan was off to such a good start.

On Sunday morning, Harry woke up late. Harry always woke up late on Sundays. He was a person who kept his routine, even when he was working on a big plan. After breakfast, Harry read the newspaper to find yard sales. He made a list of all of the addresses.

The first two yard sales were very nice, but there wasn't much to buy at either one. At the third yard sale, Harry found what he needed — a bicycle and a tricycle. He took them home and worked on his plan all day. By the end of the day, Harry was happy and a little tired. He knew that his plan was going well.

On Monday morning, Harry got an early start. After a quick but healthy breakfast, he left the house. Monday was garbage day, and Harry was hoping he would find more of the things he needed. Harry believed that you could find treasure in someone else's garbage.

Harry was thrilled when he saw the garbage can in front of Mrs. Chang's house. In it he found an old egg beater and a clothesline. These were exactly the kind of treasures Harry wanted. As soon as he got home, he started to work. He got a lot done that day. At the end of the day, Harry relaxed by watching some TV before bed.

On Tuesday morning, Harry got up very early. After breakfast, he had a shower. In the shower, he sang, he scrubbed, and he thought. Before he was done, he had a great idea. Showers often helped Harry think.

Harry hurried to The Bath Shop to buy a shower curtain. Mr. James was happy to see him. Later, at home, Harry cut strips from the curtain. Everything was going so well that Harry had time to go to the movies that night.

On Wednesday morning after breakfast, Harry went to the hardware store — his favorite kind of store. Mr. Bolt was glad to see Harry, and the two of them chatted for a long time. Harry almost forgot to buy the things he needed.

Harry checked his list to make sure that he had a mousetrap, nails, screws, nuts, and bolts. Mr. Bolt could not figure out how these things could help Harry make breakfast. But he knew better than to ask Harry. Harry liked to keep his ideas to himself. When Harry got home, he did some work. Then he started reading a new book.

On Thursday morning, Harry woke up late. He made a big breakfast and took his time eating it. He needed time to think about where to get a piece of metal. When he heard his neighbor's garage door slam shut, he knew just where to go.

Harry went to Jan's Auto Shop. Jan was happy to get him a big piece of metal. She cut it in large circles for Harry, just like he asked. Later, at home, Harry worked on the large circles until they were just right. Then he collected some more things from around the house. Harry even had time to finish reading his book.

On Friday morning, it was raining. On rainy days, Harry liked a nice, hot breakfast. He worked at home until late in the afternoon. When the rain stopped, Harry went to the grocery store.

It took Harry many trips to get the food into the car and then into his house. He was so tired that he fell asleep right away that night.

Chapter 3: Harry Makes Breakfast!

On Saturday morning, Harry woke up before sunrise. He had to get to the Fun Fair. He had just put together his invention when people started to arrive.

"Harry, what in the world have you made?" asked Mr. Bolt.

"It looks like a ride!" said Mrs. Chang.

"He's even used the shower curtains!" cried Mr. James.

"Harry, we thought you were making breakfast!" shouted everyone.

"I am," said Harry. "Watch how my breakfast-making machine works. It flips. It slides. It turns. Stand back and I'll make it go."

Harry started to pedal. He pedaled hard and fast. Everyone watched Harry and waited for the machine to start. When it did, they could not believe what they saw. It did just what Harry said.

"It flips. It slides. It turns!" everyone cheered.

In just a few minutes, people were eating a delicious breakfast.

Everyone loved watching things flip, slide, and turn. No one wanted to leave.

And because the food tasted so good, most people ate it for lunch and dinner, too.